With love on your Birthday
10TH JULY '76

Murray

Pieter Brueghel's
The Fair
Story by Ruth Craft

COLLINS · LONDON

Can you find
in the big picture
this bold man
who has climbed the tall tree?
He's found a green castle in the air.
He can see the whole fair.
He can see the world and his wife.
They're there.
And their dog.

Long ago,
Pieter Brueghel looked at a fair.
He held all the pieces quite still
in his mind's eye.
Then he painted a picture.
He painted each leaf, each head of hair.
Every hat. Every shoe.
He painted people like me and you.
He painted each eye and every ear.
Every smile. Every tear.
Like all painters,
Pieter Brueghel took his time.
Take yours.
See what you can find.

The fair is a place for meetings and greetings.
Doff your hat and wave your hand.
"Good day to you! Good day!"
The flowers are blooming
and business is booming.
"Good day to you! Good day!"

There's gossip and chatter,
chin-wag and natter.
"Did the landlord chuck you out?"
"He's been a right old so-and-so!"
"Have you made your sauerkraut?"
"Oh yes! Did that weeks ago!"
"You know that old crone Mother Jane,
well she's been telling tales again.
This time she says that Mistress Meg
keeps stacks of gold in her wooden leg!"
"Never! Do you think it's true?"
"True! True as a cat's bark or a dog's mew!"

Perhaps the man with the kind, grave face
only stopped to say,
"Hello, old friend,
and how are you today?"
Hours later Red Hat is still telling him.
"The rats got in and ate the cheese.
I fell downstairs and banged my knees.
I tore my coat on a rusty nail,
(my *best* coat, mind you, my *best* coat).
Believe me,
it's a wonder I'm alive to tell the tale."
And the man with the kind, grave face listens on. And on.

Wrinkle your nose at the fair,
and you'll sniff the whiff of hot food cooking in the air.
You'd think with hundreds of hungry to feed,
there'd be an army of cooks in a bustle.
But these four
have seen it all before,
so there's no hustle.
The boy with the basket
crashes out the empties with a rattle and a clatter.
(They're made of wood so crashing doesn't matter.)
Red Shirt and Madam White Hat
keep calm and cool.
Keep the bowls moving,
now empty, now full.
They're not rushed off their feet
just because people must eat.
And the Fireminder?
Well – he can't keep cool.
With his face like a red brick,
he pokes and stokes with his charred old stick,
so the fire will burn bright,
and keep the big pot
bubbling, steaming and piping hot.
The pigs grunt, snuffling over the ground.
There's no chance of left-overs
with sleek, greedy porkers around.

There are dozens of watchful faces around the Play.
All eyes sharp-set for a good story.
There's the Devil.
He's the one with the horns on his head
and he's whispering to the lady.
But she doesn't know that her husband is watching
because he's hiding in that basket
being carried by his friend, the pedlar.
She hasn't noticed either of them
because she's busy listening to the Devil
and he's trying to tempt her.

"Come, my pretty.
Tell a tale.
Spite a friend.
Rob a child.
Mock a believer.
Get muddled over Wrong and Right.
And play a trick as dark as any winter's night!"

"Ooooooo-er!" The crowd sighs like a furnace!
"Will she give way?
Will she live
to scorn temptation till another day?
And, what's more, what's her husband going to say?"

Look closely.
There's someone else in another kind of play.
A cruel play.
For come what may,
this poor cripple must show off his pain every day.
Nobody claps him,
or praises his show.
Some stop to give a little,
some nothing – and go.

Some people will sit anywhere to see a good show.
Safe as houses?
The two on the ridge of the roof
will come to no harm
especially with the friendly fence of a good strong arm.

As for old Clever Boots
in his smart white pants,
he'd be safer dancing
with a herd of elephants.
For what if a rumble
should start off a tumble?
And what if the tumble
should start off a fall?
And what if that fall
should start off a crash?
And what if that crash
should end in a splash?
Splish, splosh, splash!
If he falls in the soup
he'll look a right nincompoop!

Today is Saint's Day, Fair Day, Holiday.
Sweet as a nut.
Tomorrow is work day, chore day, worry day.
Back in the rut.

Follow the dancing leader round.
This way?
No – that!
Whoops! There's no turning back.
The leader spins the dancers round
like a skipping rope skimming across the ground.

Jig-a-jogger up!
Jig-a-jogger down!
Jig-a-jogger fill your cup
And jig round the town.

Boom-tiddle-tiddle-boom cha cha!
Boom-tiddle-tiddle-boom!
Pick up your toes in time to the tune.
Swing round your partners;
Give your elbows some room.
Boom-tiddle-tiddle-boom cha cha!
Boom-tiddle-tiddle-boom!

Sing a Hosanna!
Hold high the brave banners!
As high as the tree,
for the whole world to see.

To remember the Saints and honour their souls,
their fine carved statues clothed in crimson and gold
are carried with pride through the loud jubilee.
And the strong men who hold them,
hold them carefully.

For today is the birthday of the Saints.
And you know
the saints were good men of God,
who died long ago.

Follow the drum . . .
Hey-diddle-dum,
Diddle-dum, diddle-dum.
Who follows the drum?
Whose marching feet
follow the drummer's beat?

Six fine archers,
ready to go!
Ready at a stroke
to draw back their bows –
Zing!
So the arrows will fly
like flocks of starlings in a clear blue sky.
Who'll be the winner?
Who's game to say
who'll shoot the furthest and fastest today?

No fair is a fair without the Fool . . .
Who follows him?

A fool in those days of long, long ago,
was proud to tread on a swanky toe.
A sparky, sharp and nimble-witted fellow
whose clothes were coloured red and yellow.
With his wit and wisdom,
this canny clown
is paid to turn the gloomy world
right upside down.

Jingle-a-ringle,
his whirly-gig spins.
His coat flaps behind him
and the children join in.

"Tom Fool, Tom Fool.
We'll chase you all day.
We'll hang on your coat
And we won',t go away.
Tom Fool, Tom Fool.
Sing us the rhyme
Of the cat who fished frogs
With the green washing line."

At a big, busy rowdy fair
it's safer to stick together.
Even if it does lead to arguments.
One wants to go one way.
And one, the other.
"I want to see Tom Fool.
He's over there."
"And I want to see the Play
and *that's* over there."
"I'm not leaving *you* alone.
Last time you got lost.
And you cried.
And we had to go home."
"Well, this time I won't.
I promise. True."

So! What are they going to do?

You have to sit down sometimes to get something
sorted out once and for all.

This soft white hat,
it won't do.
A floppy hat,
or a loose shoe,
can slow you down
when you've things to do.
Now hat,
stay firm.
Stay tight.
I can't stop every minute to put you right.

The fair is a place for buying and selling . . .

Who will buy?
And what will they buy?
Who'll come home with no money today?
"It's a bargain! A snip!" the stallholders cry.
"You won't do better wherever you try!"
But the shoppers need time
to make up their minds.
Will they buy . . .
A trinket for a birthday?
Some lace for their wife?
A stout cooking kettle
to last them all their life?
Some wooden bowls? A locket?
Or a sharp new knife?

How to decide?
You might get taken for a ride.
You could end up broke
with a pig in a poke!

Chop! Chop!
Chop on the block!
Chop the dried meat
into chunky chops.
The customers argue and haggle and mock,
"That piece looks rotten – as tough as a rock!"
The butcher snarls,
"Oh Balderdash!
Don't give me that!
Go and chew your fancy hat!"

Here's a bunch of nasties!

Bully boys have been the same since time began.
Old Squashed Face doesn't need to be told that.
He's just praying they'll sort out their argy-bargy
and get off his poor legs.

But Yellow Jacket and Red Nose are hard at it.
"Cheat! Scrounger!"
"Blackguard! Stinking egg!"
"Oh do lay off!" thinks Squashed Face.
"And do get off my *legs*!"

Blue Jacket takes on all comers.
"Bet you can't beat that!
Bet you can't win!
Bet you can't poke your ear with your chin!"

He gets as good as he gives.
"Bet I can!
Bet I can!
Bet I'll fry your nose in the frying pan!"

There's so much going on at the table you can't blame
White Suit for thinking he might get away with it!

Whisper a secret to your sweet pet.
Drain the round jug to the last drop.
Shake firm hands. It's a bet!
Turn your back? Whoops! It's a fair cop!
"Lay off! Who do you think you are? Crawling round tables
in your best white suit! You try that again, my lad,
and I'll give you such a wallop you won't know whether
it's Christmas or Thursday!"

The old dog knows better.
Patience. Patience.
Stick around. Someone will throw him a bone and then he
can take it off and get on with it in peace and quiet.
He knows there's no point in stealing from tables.
That's a puppy's trick.

Knees, elbows, noses, chins,
jam-packed together,
round the table in the inn.
Some want this,
and some want that.
If you're not very careful
your soup slops in your lap.
Jiggle elbows carefully,
then you can be sure
the spoon will land inside your mouth
and not inside your ear!

Well away from all the crush
and guzzling on her own,
Brown-eyes-pick-the-pies
chews on her bone.

There's always somebody who leaves everything
to the last minute.
Still, better late than never.

"Come on, slowcoach!
What took you so long?
Get moving, old snail,
you're just like the cow's tail,
always behind!
Budge up everybody!
There's room for one more.
It's a bit of a squeeze,
but he's worth waiting for."
Pile up the wagon.
It's time to go.
Pack up the load
and make for the road.

But hold your horses!
Whoah!
You don't have to go.
Leave the Fair?
Never!
The picture is here forever.

"The Village Fair" was painted by Pieter Brueghel the Younger. He is known as the Younger because his father, also called Pieter, was a painter, and later his own son Pieter was called Pieter Brueghel the Third.

Pieter Brueghel the Younger was born in Brussels in 1564. By the time he was fourteen both his parents were dead and Pieter, his younger brother Jan (who also became a painter) and his sister Marie were taken to live with their grandmother in Antwerp. Their grandmother was herself a painter and it was she who encouraged and taught Pieter until he was accepted by a Guild as a "Son of a Master" in 1585. In those days a young painter had to have a long training and apprenticeship in order to become a member of the Guild. The Guilds were powerful groups of workers who came together to protect the reputations of craftsmen and artists and to keep the standards of work as high as possible.

Pieter spent much of his life copying the works of his father from engravings and drawings left behind. But "The Village Fair" is one of his own paintings. He made many versions of it and the one used in this book can be found in the Musées Royaux des Beaux-Arts in Brussels. There are other versions in museums in Vienna, Amsterdam and Cambridge, England.

Pieter Brueghel the Younger had many pupils and he was teaching right up to his death in 1638 at the age of 74.

William Collins Sons & Co Ltd
London · Glasgow · Sydney · Auckland
Toronto · Johannesburg

"The Village Fair" by Pieter Brueghel reproduced by permission of
The Musées Royaux des Beaux-Arts, Brussels, Belgium

Designed by John Trevitt
First published 1975
Text © Ruth Craft 1975

ISBN 0 00 183719-2

Phototypeset by Tradespools Ltd, Frome, Somerset
Made and Printed in Great Britain by
W. S. Cowell Ltd, Ipswich